To my teenage girls, Hannah and Lola,
for putting my life on Earth in perspective —CB

To Mom and Dad, with love —SW

For my son Sebastian—my shining star in the sky —AH

Quarto is the authority on a wide range of topics.

Quarto educates, entertains and enriches the lives of
our readers—enthusiasts and lovers of hands-on living.

www.quartoknows.com

**The publishers and authors would like to thank
Monica Grady, Professor of Planetary and Space Science at the Open University,
for her invaluable advice and support as a scientific consultant for this book.**

Text copyright © Catherine Barr and Steve Williams 2017
Illustrations copyright © Amy Husband 2017

First published in the USA in 2017 by
Frances Lincoln Children's Books, an imprint of Quarto Inc.,
142 W 36th St, 4th Floor, New York, NY 10018, USA
QuartoKnows.com
Visit our blogs at QuartoKnows.com

ISBN 978-1-78603-003-0

Illustrated with mixed media and collage

Set in Gill Sans

Printed in China

9 8 7 6 5 4 3 2 1

MIX
Paper from
responsible sources
FSC® C008047

The Story of
SPACE

A first book about our universe

I'm off to explore the beginning of time...

Wait for me!

Catherine Barr and **Steve Williams**
Illustrated by **Amy Husband**

Frances Lincoln
Children's Books

Before the Big Bang, there was nothing at all.

No galaxies, no stars, no planets, and no life.
No time, no space, no light, and no sound.

Then, suddenly, it all began.

dark energy

Where did THAT come from?

13.8 billion years ago

Milky Way

supermassive black hole

This blisteringly hot blast began to cool.

Bits from the blast formed tiny things called atoms, which made gas and dust. The gas twisted and clumped, getting hotter and hotter until it burned and shone.

13.8–13.1 billion years ago

Deneb

blue-white star

Regulus

white supergiant

Polaris

yellow supergiant

Over time, trillions of stars lit up the universe. Like us, stars are born, grow old, and die. Unlike us, they live for billions of years, so many of these first stars still sparkle today.

During their lifetimes, stars twinkle in rainbow colors. The hottest look blueish, while cooler stars are white, yellow, and red. Really big stars are called giants, and smaller ones are called dwarfs. Dwarf red stars are the most common of all.

13.1–4.5 billion years ago

When they die, some stars grow into huge red giants before shrinking back to white dwarfs that fade and disappear. Other massive stars explode and collapse into strange black holes that suck everything inward.

Aldebaran

Betelgeuse

orange-red giant

red supergiant

They're so colorful!

A very long time after the Big Bang, a bright yellow star, our sun, was born.
This burning ball of gas is so huge that over a million Earths would fit inside it.

The sun is incredibly hot, with a fiery furnace in its core. Cooler black spots shift across its surface. A fierce solar wind loops and flows outward toward deep space.

Our sun is just one of billions of stars in our galaxy, the Milky Way.

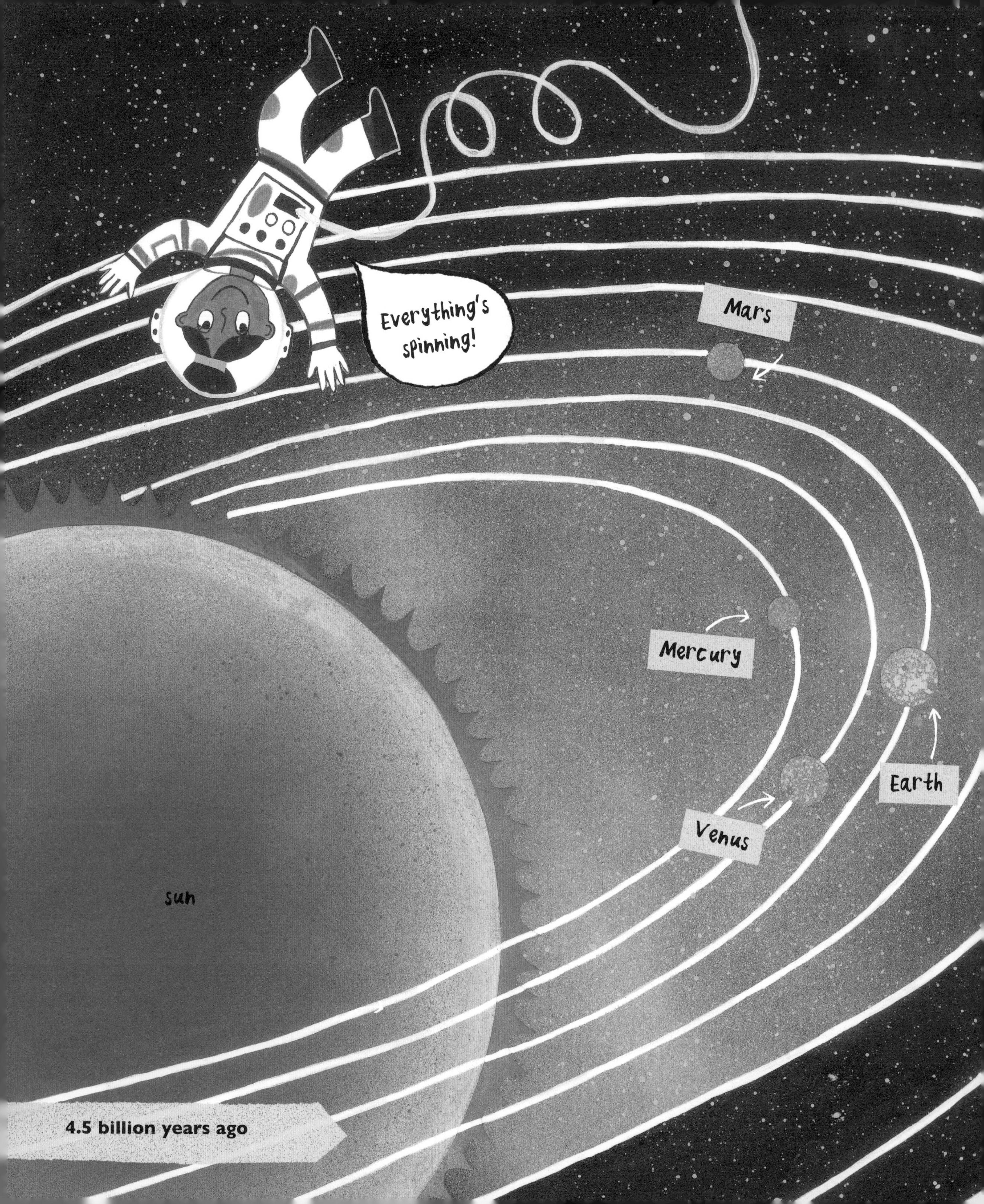

4.5 billion years ago

deep space

Neptune

Jupiter

Uranus

Saturn

Over time, dust and gas left over from the birth of the sun clumped together to make planets.

Close to the sun, dust formed the rocky planets of Mercury, Venus, Earth, and Mars. In the icy blackness far from the sun's warm glow, Jupiter, Saturn, Uranus, and Neptune were made from dust swirling with gas and ice.

All these new planets whizzed at breathtaking speeds around their yellow star. Our solar system had been born.

It's making me dizzy!

comets

Whooa! That's MASSIVE!

As well as planets, lumps of rock and ice called comets hurtled around the sun.

Asteroids, made of chunks of rock and metal, also circled the sun. Many of these crashed into the Earth's surface. They made it so hot that the rocks melted into endlessly bubbling lakes of lava.

Soon after Earth was formed, a planet-sized asteroid ripped through space and smashed into the globe. Rocks blasted off into space, eventually sticking together to become our cold, dusty moon.

4.5 billion years ago

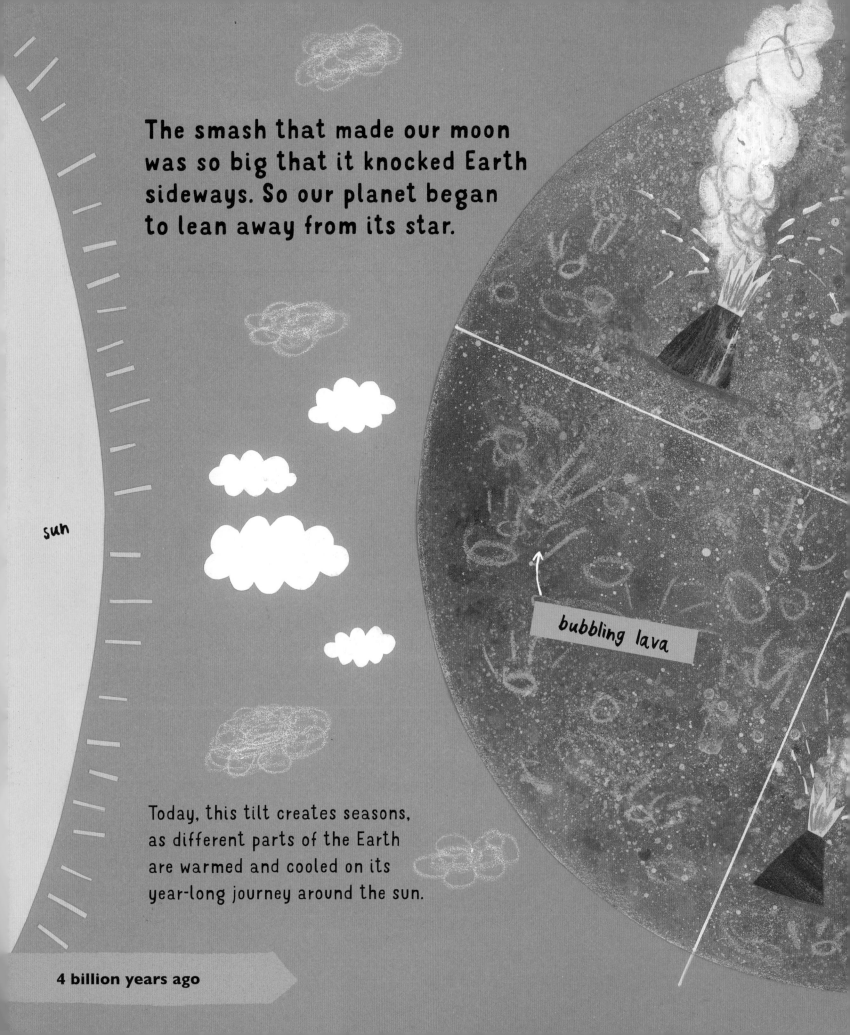

The smash that made our moon was so big that it knocked Earth sideways. So our planet began to lean away from its star.

sun

Today, this tilt creates seasons, as different parts of the Earth are warmed and cooled on its year-long journey around the sun.

bubbling lava

4 billion years ago

As the Earth spins on its axis, different areas endlessly turn toward and away from the sun. This creates cycles of night and day around the world.

Temperatures on Earth began to drop, and its surface of boiling lava cooled to solid rock.

It rained for thousands of years, creating vast oceans. In these seas, the first forms of life appeared. These early cells began to produce oxygen, the gas we all breathe today.

Earth today

3.8 billion years ago—today

As oxygen spread across the globe, it triggered an explosion of life that lasted for billions of years.

Sometimes asteroids and comets smashed into Earth, almost destroying all living things. But incredibly, some animals and plants survived and have flourished. Just three million years ago, new animals evolved that are changing the world: humans!

Jupiter

I'm glad we live there.

Life on Earth depends on our atmosphere, the thin blanket of gases that wraps around the globe and traps warmth and the oxygen that humans and other living things need.

But in space, it is bitterly cold with no air. The atmospheres of other planets are freezing, poisonous, suffocating, or all three. Venus has yellow acid fog, while bolts of lightning shoot through red storms on Jupiter. Saturn has rings of ice and raging orange winds. Humans are still trying to understand these planets and everything that spins around them.

Astronomers first explored space by gazing at the stars—and invented telescopes to help them study the skies.

They found craters on the moon and discovered Saturn's rings. They realized that the universe is mysterious and constantly changing. But over time, they began to explain and understand it using math and maps.

Astronomers mapped the stars in our galaxy, the Milky Way, and gazed at billions of other galaxies stretching like cobwebs across the sky. They saw moons orbiting planets and planets orbiting stars.

Astronomers figured out that everything in the universe is controlled by strange forces.

Dark energy is still pushing everything in space apart, while gravity pulls everything together. The more massive the object, the stronger its gravity.

black hole

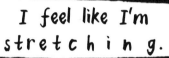

On Earth, gravity stops
us from falling off the planet.
In space, it tugs planets
around stars and forms
galaxies by pulling stars
around supermassive black holes.

Black holes are strange, dark places
where gravity is strongest of all—so
powerful that even light gets sucked in.

Laika the dog

Earth

1942-1969

Eventually scientists figured out how to escape Earth's gravity—by blasting off in a rocket. The Space Race had begun.

First animals, then people were strapped in for the ride. The first man sent into space was named Yuri, and the first woman was Valentina, both from Russia. It took them less than two hours to orbit the globe.

Then, in 1969, the world held its breath while the American Apollo 11 space mission set off to do something new and extraordinary—land on the moon.

The astronauts wriggled out of the small door of the Eagle spacecraft. For the first time, they stood on something in the universe other than Earth.

footprints

They could bounce up and down on the powdery surface because the moon, being a lot smaller than Earth, has weak gravity. The astronauts had practiced in swimming pools in their space suits, because floating in water is a bit like walking on the moon.

1969

The astronauts took photographs, collected moon dust, and phoned home. They left footprints in the dust, and undisturbed by air or water, these human marks remain. But the astronauts themselves rocketed home to planet Earth.

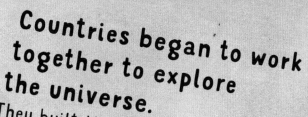

Countries began to work together to explore the universe. They built the International Space Station, where people carry out all sorts of experiments in outer space.

Spacecraft with robots have landed on Venus, Mars, and even on a comet. Space probes have orbited Mercury, Saturn, and Jupiter, while others still rocket on a one-way ticket into deep space.

Hundreds of satellites orbit the Earth. Some are human space trash. But others take pictures that help us understand the weather and bounce signals to Earth that make televisions and telephones work.

space junk

1970s–today

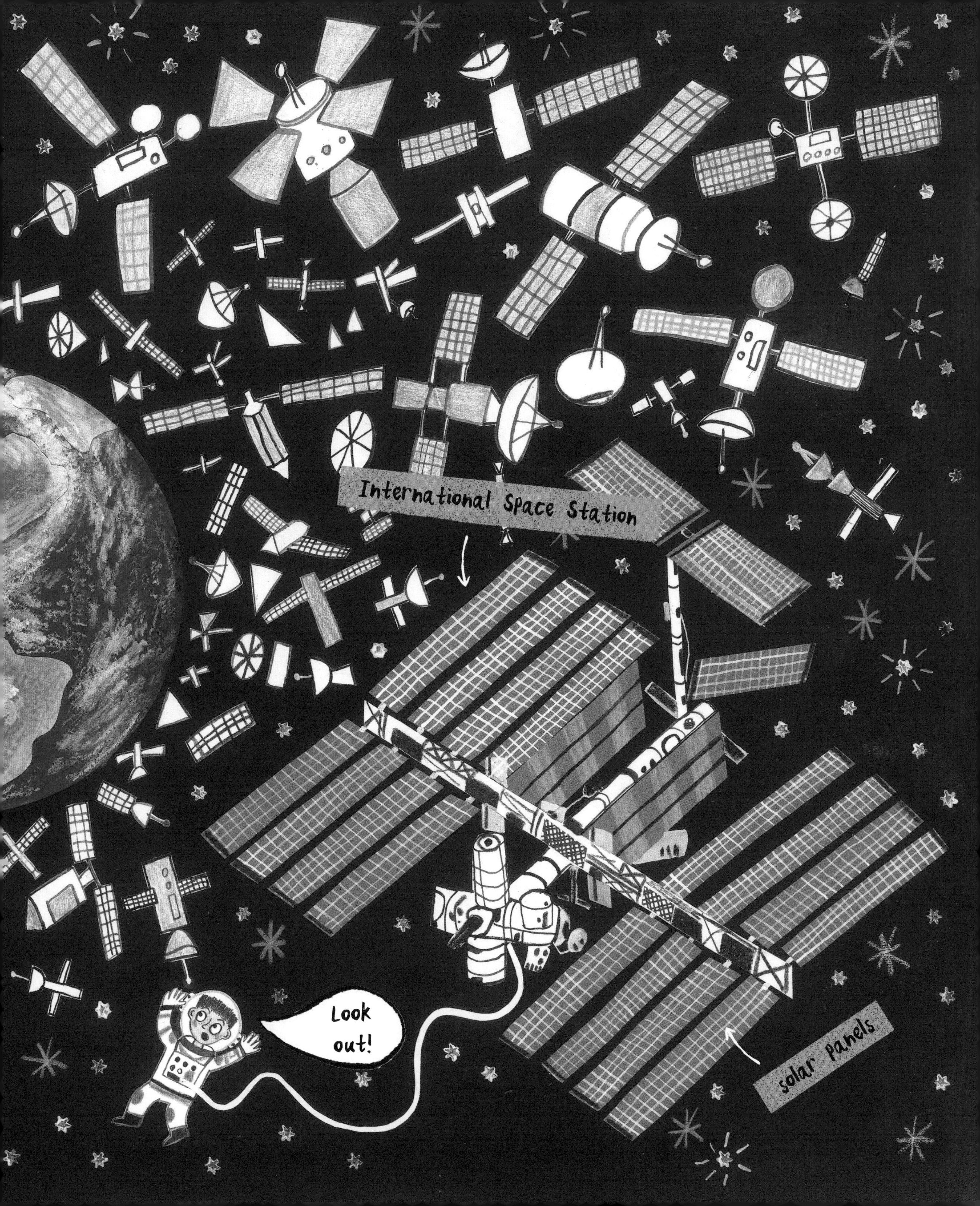
International Space Station
solar panels
Look out!

The biggest challenges to exploring space are time and distance. Just to reach the edge of our own galaxy would take about four billion years.

Soon, spaceships will be built so that people can rocket off on vacation, and astronauts hope to land and survive on Mars.

the future

Good-bye, everyone.
We're off!

deep space

Mars

space hotel

One of the most
exciting challenges of
all is to search other moons and
planets for signs of life. It is unlikely
that we are totally alone.

No one knows what we will find as we unravel the
mysteries of the extraordinary place we call space.

Glossary of useful words

Asteroid – a lump of rock and metal that orbits the sun.

Astronaut – someone who visits and explores space.

Astronomer – someone who studies the stars and the planets.

Atoms – the smallest building blocks for everything in the universe.

Big Bang – the moment when time and space began, making our universe.

Black hole – a place in outer space where gravity is so strong that even light gets sucked in.

Dark energy – a force created by the Big Bang that is still pushing everything in the universe outward.

Comet – a ball of ice, dust, and rock that orbits the sun, growing a tail of dust and ice as it comes closer toward the sun.

Galaxy – billions of stars, gas, and dust held together by gravity.

Gravity – a force that pulls things toward each other.

Milky Way – our own galaxy of stars that includes our solar system.

Moon – an object that orbits a planet.

Orbit – the curved path of one object around another.

Oxygen – a gas that makes up about a fifth of our atmosphere, which gives most living things the energy to survive and grow.

Satellite – an object that moves around another object in space.

Solar System – our sun and everything orbiting it, including Earth.

Star – a ball of very hot gas giving off the energy that creates light.

Universe – a space formed by the Big Bang, which includes everything that exists.